Woman, Wife, Mother

Great Moms Are Made

Written by

Akhere Ugbo

Copyright © 2017 by Akhere Ugbo

VMH Vikki M. Hankins™ Publishing
3355 Lenox Rd. NE Suite 750 Atlanta, GA 30331
www.vmhpublishing.com

Without limiting the rights under copyright reserved above, no part of this publication may be reproduced, stored in or introduced into a retrieval system, or transmitted, in any form or by any means, without prior written permission of both the copyright owner and publisher of this book. Your support of the author's rights is appreciated.

ISBN: 978-1-94792823-7

10 9 8 7 6 5 4 3 2 1

Publisher's Note:

The publisher is not responsible for the content of this book nor websites, or social media pages (or their content) that are not owned by the publisher.

DEDICATION

To GOD Almighty for giving me the wisdom to build my home; to my wonderful and amiable parents, for nurturing me into the woman that I have become today; to my amazingly sweet husband, the love of my life, and my adorable children with beautiful hearts, thank you so much for making my roles as a wife, and a mother much easier than I would have ever imagined; to my dear twin sister and awesome brothers, for being a wonderful part of my beautiful story.

PREFACE

Every woman is unique. A woman someday becomes a wife, and then; a mom - Awesome! This book focuses on helping every woman become the best wife and mom she can possibly be, while taking advantage of the uniqueness that makes her stand out. It helps moms experience the beauty of motherhood. First and foremost, it deals extensively with teaching women about the importance of choosing the right spouse, which is the first and most important step to a happy and fulfilled home. Besides helping moms discover how to enjoy motherhood, it takes into mind the fact that GOD – who created us for specific reasons – has given each person the ability to successfully achieve that purpose accordingly. This book also creates ways to help women discover much about themselves and their abilities, while encouraging them to put their expertise to good use. It teaches them the need to

PREFACE

set their priorities right and how to go about doing so; and it teaches them to stick with whatever produces the best outcome for them in any given situation. It also encourages moms to be successful in their dealings both inside and outside the home. However, moms must wisely strike a balance between the two, so that they are successful in both situations. It reminds us of the importance of good parenting even while pursuing a career. It provides substantial insight into what cheating on a spouse is all about and the need to keep love alive. It encourages moms to pay the necessary price of motherhood in order to reap the full benefits in later years. Finally, and most importantly, it admonishes every mom to put her home first, while making other dealings "complementary," so they do not lead to the complete "neglect" of her home.

CONTENTS

Preface	5
Introduction	9
1. The Right Spouse	17
2. A Woman's Role as a Wife and as a Mom	41
3. Self-Discovery and Development	63
4. Nurture Your Children with a Sense of Purpose	75
5. Set Your Priorities Right	91
6. Take a Break	97
7. Career and Parenting	101
8. A Cheating Spouse	115
9. When Love Dies… and Why?	125
10. Paying the Price	133
11. Lasting Fulfillment	141
12. Actions Speak Louder…	149
Conclusion	165

INTRODUCTION

As a young woman, I never thought about finding out what being a wife entailed. I felt being a wife was effortless because it seemed quite easy for my mom. Now I know differently.

As a teenager, I once thought that being a mom was the easiest thing to do. On the contrary, it is about the most difficult thing I have ever done. Yet, with no doubt in my heart, it is by far the sweetest and most amazing experience of a life time.

I am a very thorough person. Initially as a new mom, I found it very difficult to cope with the demands of motherhood because of that trait, but overtime; I learned to strike a balance between everything. Motherhood has not changed my personality one bit; it has only made me a much better person. Although I am still a young mom, I look back in time, and it seems as though I have been on this journey for decades, primarily because

INTRODUCTION

of the necessary changes which I had to make in my life. For me, motherhood is an endless journey with life-changing experiences. It is the most beautiful and rewarding experience any woman could ever have. Apart from motherhood moulding me into a much better person, it has made me view life with a totally different perspective.

Permit me to briefly mention the many benefits of motherhood:

1. As a mom you must be excellent at multitasking because you have no other option than to handle more than one task at the same time in order to get all of the things done that need doing, and just in time. With time, multitasking becomes routine.

2. The multiple roles assumed by moms range from being a wife to a nanny, cook, cleaner, gardener, teacher, nurse, time-keeper, counsellor, chauffeur, security officer, tailor and more. In no time, you acquire so much

knowledge and so many more skills than you could have ever imagined from playing those roles.

3. The need for flexibility becomes a necessity as following your own schedule may not always be possible. Flexibility helps to keep one's sanity intact.

4. It makes us more responsible and hardworking individuals.

5. It makes us more vigilant about what goes on around us.

6. The numerous challenges we face each day prepare us for much bigger challenges that come our way; with every experience and conquered challenge, our problem solving and organizational skills are increased.

7. It enables us to be the closest person to our children, and it helps us to know even the tiniest details about them. It gives mothers the privilege of being the first or perhaps the

INTRODUCTION

only person to know the secrets of their children. Children also tend to make their moms their confidant. In most cases, mothers could become middle-men between the children and their fathers.

I could go on and on about the numerous benefits of motherhood. As I go on, you will get to see, appreciate and learn more about these benefits. I call them benefits because in one way or another, our lives are shaped by all these numerous activities and responsibilities. Not to mention the added advantage of the brain being kept active all day long.

As mothers, we have an inner strength which is innate (God created us that way). Bear in mind that God did not make any mistake creating women. He was indeed deliberate. If you, as a woman, did not have the capacity to face the challenges of motherhood, then you would have no business being a woman. In essence, every

INTRODUCTION

woman has the capacity to go through this beautiful journey of motherhood. The difference lies in how we go about it.

I go through each day by the special grace of God. To be honest with you, so many times I thought it was impossible to go on. The responsibilities just kept popping up without an end in sight. I asked myself how others were handling these responsibilities without falling apart. Sometimes, I got extremely tired, so tired I would rather call it being 'tiyahd' (a neologism of mine to refer to extreme tiredness).

Other young moms that I spoke with often voiced a subtle feeling of despair about how tedious their tasks were. It was present in almost every conversation I had with them. Ironically, I always had words of encouragement for them, which always made them feel better. It took me quite a while to come to the realization that it was not about me, but about God. He gave me

INTRODUCTION

the responsibility of motherhood and He is indeed capable of seeing me through it. I decided to stop focusing on the tasks and responsibilities I had to face as a mom, and start developing myself into a much better person. I started focusing more on the positive than on the negative. I started drawing my strength from within instead of from the prevailing circumstances around me. Finally, I decided to make the prevailing circumstances work for me and not against me. In other words, I stopped allowing the challenges of motherhood to define my existence. You can either allow the challenges of motherhood to weigh you down or you can rise above them and make them work to your advantage. The choice is yours.

Do not for once think that you can make it through this life changing journey on your own. Many women have failed in their responsibilities as wives and mothers, not because they wanted to, but because they failed

INTRODUCTION

to recognize the true source of their strength, GOD – Our Creator. Some women have gone insane trying to make it on their own. A few others can no longer recognize themselves. They have become monsters to themselves, their spouses, their children and everyone around them. Many more are on the verge of having a nervous breakdown. Really! We do not see these things happening around us because we moms are too busy trying to put and keep our homes together. No mom can conveniently talk about how tasking her responsibilities are because the world would judge her and see her as an outright failure, which forces so many moms to bottle up their emotions. When they can no longer take it, they explode! Why get to the point of having a nervous breakdown when it can be avoided.

This book thus transcends helping you experience the true beauty of motherhood, to moulding you into the wife and mother you

INTRODUCTION

were created to be, while motivating you to go through each day with the right attitude. Enjoy it!

1

THE RIGHT SPOUSE

A glove should always fit perfectly in order for the hand to function without difficulties. So also should be the case of a spouse.

Getting it right, that is, making the right choice of a husband can be likened to looking before you leap. If you leap before you look, be prepared to face and accept whatever challenges you meet on the other side. This chapter deals mainly with getting it right before marriage and getting married to the right spouse. I deliberately chose to put this chapter first because I do not want to put the cart before the horse.

Marriage is no competition, but it involves team work. Hence, having the right teammate on board is critical to sustaining any marriage. A team is any group of people involved in the same activity, who share the same interest and look out for each other. A teammate is someone who is on the same team. An opponent is on an opposing team. An opponent is a rival, and does not share the same interest as his rival, and attempts to stop his rival's progress. In a marriage, it is extremely important to have a teammate on board and not an opponent, for obvious reasons. Teammates are never in competition with one another. They are always expected to work together for the good of their team.

Words cannot describe the importance of having the right spouse. One should never get married just for the sake of it. Rather, you should ensure that you settle down for the right reasons. You may not necessarily hear from God concerning who the spouse should be. If you invite God into your relationship from the outset, while taking care to do the right things, He will certainly not abandon you, but order your footsteps accordingly.

In essence, getting it right is the *ultimate* and most important step in achieving a healthy, happy, sustainable and successful marriage. No one would want to spend the rest of her life going through the trauma of trying to fix a bad marriage as a result of a bad choice, when making the right choice is not so difficult. Prevention they say is better than cure. Notwithstanding, whether you get it or got it right or wrong, there is absolutely no doubt that being a wife as well as a mom comes with its numerous challenges but, it is certainly a lot easier to go through these challenges with the right spouse/teammate. It is therefore, the responsibility of every woman who intends to get married to do her homework properly and well before hand. Meaning, a young girl would have to develop herself spiritually, intellectually, physically, and otherwise, to become the right person for the right man, known as "Mr. Right," who is someone who complements you. You will get to know a lot about self-development in chapter three of this book. Mark my words: I said Mr. Right, and not Mr. Perfect. Do not be misled, no one is perfect.

Every prospective mom must be spiritually, physically and psychologically (that is mentally and emotionally) prepared for the journey of motherhood. It is definitely not for the faint-hearted. Do not get me wrong, I am not trying to frighten prospective mothers. I am only being very honest with them. I am using the word 'prospective' because not every woman intends to get married or settle down. The word 'prospective' therefore defines those who are willing to become moms someday. Back to my point, the right state of mind is attainable only if the right things are put in place and the right choices are made very early in one's life. It is important to note that the challenges faced by every mom are particular to each mom, and as such cannot be compared with those faced by any other mom on this planet. Challenges could appear similar, but the circumstances surrounding every challenge definitely differ for different moms.

Challenges faced by moms range from the chores in the house to attending to the needs of the children, minding her job or business, attending to the needs of her spouse and so on. Some other moms may also have the additional burden of having to deal with the infidelity of their spouses (see chapters seven and eight of this book). Before going further, I must categorically state that no marriage is perfect, and no two marriages are similar. Each of them depends on the circumstances surrounding the couple; but, every Christian union has been blessed by God **(Genesis 1:27-28 GNB):**

> **Verse 27: So God created human beings, making them to be like himself. He created them male and female**
>
> **Verse 28: blessed them, and said, "Have many children, so that your descendants will live all over the earth and bring it under their control..."**

It is a known fact that God does not attach sorrow, ill-luck or misfortune to His blessings.

The blessing of the LORD brings rich, and He adds no sorrow to it (Proverbs 10:22 AMP).

As I stated earlier, choosing the right spouse is the ultimate, and indeed, the first step to a very successful and fulfilling marriage. When a wrong choice is made, everything goes wrong. Only the timely intervention of God can save a wrong marriage from becoming a total disaster. Wait a minute! Why would anyone want to go through fixing a wrong decision when it could be avoided completely? "Prevention" is the key word. As a matter of great concern, I urge every woman intending to enter the institution of marriage to seek the face of God; because God has never and will never make a mistake. **"If you ask me anything in my name, I will do it"** (John 14:14 AMP). "Anything" includes God's help in meeting the right spouse. It is extremely important to get it right because *forever* is a really long time. For so many, John 14:14 may sound cliché, but remember, it is God's word! God's word has never failed, and it will never fail concerning you or your circumstances. Trust God for the right spouse and He will surely grant your heart's desires. By the special grace of God, I am a living testimony of the goodness of God. He answered my heart's desires and can also answer yours, if only you will trust in Him. Why take chances when you can get it right on the first attempt with the help of GOD. **The words and promises of the LORD are pure words, Like silver refined in an earthen furnace, purified seven times (Psalm 12:6 AMP).** That is not to say that having the right spouse makes it challenge-free. But, it certainly makes it a lot easier to face whatever challenges that may come along. Every woman deserves and needs the support of her spouse, whether voiced or implied, and a shoulder to lean on whenever the need arises. She should know that she has a cheerleader to cheer her on even in the most difficult of circumstances. This certainly encourages and propels her to do a lot more than she would ever be capable of doing on her own. How can one be inspired to excel or succeed, or even strive to put in her best in life in a tense and hostile environment, or in an unhappy state of mind?

One solemn point which many often neglect is the aspect of "abstinence before marriage." If you trust God for a spouse, then you must be ready to obey God's word in the issue of abstinence **(1st Corinthians 6:13 & 18).** For the sake of clarity, abstinence before marriage has to do with staying away from sex (keeping your body holy and untouched); it is *total*. Some people erroneously believe that abstinence does not have to be total. They have redefined abstinence to suit themselves. They believe that a person can still engage in some form of sexual activities such as kissing, caressing or some other form of foreplay. That is a very big lie from the pit of hell. Foreplay is a recommended prerequisite for sex. They are activities that take place before people have sex. It is advisable to avoid everything that has to do with sex. I would buttress my point with the following verses of the Bible **(GNB)**:

> **1st Corinthians 6:13: ...The body is not to be used for sexual immorality, but to serve the Lord; and the Lord provides for the body.**
>
> **1st Corinthians 6:18: Avoid immorality. Any other sin a man commits does not affect his body; but the man who is guilty of sexual immorality sins against his own body.**
>
> **1st Corinthians 6:19: Don't you know that your body is the temple of the Holy Spirit, who lives in you and who was given to you by God? You do not belong to yourselves but to God.**

> **1st Corinthians 7:2: But because there is so much immorality, every man should have his own wife, and every woman should have her own husband.**

When you start sleeping with whom you are in a relationship with, you have directly and indirectly shut God out of your life. Directly; by sinning against your body, you sin against God. Indirectly; by telling God that you have chosen your spouse and that His opinion does not matter, because God permits sex only within the institution of marriage. See **1st Corinthians 7:2 supra.** In other words, sex can only be carried out exclusively by married couples. If you take it on yourself to do God's job, you will have only yourself to blame for any mishaps afterwards. What I mean by "doing God's job" is this: when you decide to have sex or even go as far as cohabiting with the person you are in a relationship with, then your actions imply that you have chosen a spouse for yourself and that you do not need the help of God. It is as simple as that!

Many may argue that some people have been successful in their marriages by engaging in such unholy acts before marriage. Do not be too sure about that! It only seems so. You do not know the price some may have paid or are still paying for that act of immorality. **Galatians 6:7-8 (GNB): Do not deceive yourselves; no one makes a fool of God. People will reap exactly what they sow. If they sow in the field of their natural desires, from it they will gather the harvest of death; if they sow in the field of the spirit, from the spirit they will gather the harvest of eternal life.** Many of these people have to live with the regrets of their past. Many more are battling with health issues; while a lot more are an "emotional wreck," and are merely just existing and finding it very difficult to live a fulfilled life. Be very sincere with yourself. What do you really want to make out of your life? Do you want to allow God to have His way, or do you want to go ahead and do it your way? The choice is yours.

A certain young man whom I had known since childhood, but had never had a close relationship with, ran into me in my final year at the University. He wanted to enter into a relationship with me, but I put him off. I told him that we would be better off as friends for the time being because I had a lot of work to do that particular year and did not want to be distracted. To cut the long story short, we finally got into a relationship after my graduation from school. Just a little while into our relationship, he made a suggestion to become intimate. I asked, feigning ignorance, what he meant by that. He said something of this sort: "You know now!" I replied to him by saying that I did not know what he was talking about. I was deliberate in acting as if I was naive. I said that we spoke and saw each other frequently enough and that was enough intimacy for me. He smiled at me. At that point, I could no longer hold back. I carefully explained to him why a young woman ought to keep her body a living sacrifice to God. I remember telling him that I wanted to be able to stand before God in prayer without feeling any sense of guilt. I wanted to be able to pray to God and know that He would answer my prayers.

While I was in that relationship, I was constantly on my knees asking God to reveal to me who the young man really was. I did not want to rely on the mere fact that we had known each other's backgrounds to some extent. For me, marriage was and still is a very big deal. I did not want to spend the rest of my life with the wrong person. I knew that it was only by the help of God that I could achieve that. If I wanted God to help me in that regard, then I also had a duty to remain a sanctuary, pure and holy, tried and true. Precisely three months into our relationship, God made a stunning revelation to me concerning the young man - he was not who or what he had claimed to be. I did not need a soothsayer to realize that. God did it! That was all I needed. Of course, I quit the relationship with my integrity still intact, by the special grace of

God. Every woman should endeavour to take a stand in every relationship she finds herself in, without being disrespectful about it, regardless of what happens afterwards.

I say "regardless" because it leads me to another interesting true life story about a young woman whose male friend ended their relationship because she did not want to become intimate with him. For the purpose of clarity, the word "intimacy," as used by the two young men in both stories, refers to "sexual relationship." According to him, he loved her very much (so he claimed), but he felt that by being intimate, they would get much closer. The questions she asked him during the course of the whole episode gladdened my heart. The conversation below gives a picture of what may have ensued between both parties:

Miss A: How about your ex-girlfriend?

Mr. B: What do you mean?

Miss A: I thought you said you were intimate with her.

Mr. B: Yes I was; so?

Miss A: Then why did you break up with her?

I cannot recall precisely the answer he gave, but to cut the long story short, they broke up! She cried so much about it. At first, I could not understand why she made a fuss about the break up. She said she could not give him what he was asking for because she was still a virgin. Yet, she cried her eyes out. Then I realized that she had obviously fallen in love with the wrong person. Nonetheless, thank GOD she did the right thing in the end. Today, she is happily married. The bottom line is that God's word has said it all in **1st Corinthians 6:18 (KJV): Flee fornication.** The word 'flee' means to run away; to escape; to vanish; to disappear quickly. However any young woman can flee, she should just do it because being outside of God's will is a very terrible place to be. Women – Obey God's word!

If anyone feels she may have made a wrong choice of a spouse due to certain wrong decisions she might have made in the past, the good news is that you have an obligation to make your marriage work for your own good, that of your spouse and the children, if any. **Proverbs 14:1 (GNB): "Homes are made by the wisdom of women, but are destroyed by foolishness."** Pray to God for the wisdom to attain or to maintain a healthy, happy, long lasting marriage. Every woman must cultivate the habit of taking every issue in her marriage to God in prayer. Talk less about your issues and pray more about them. Stop taking your disagreements outside of the three most important people in the institution of marriage –GOD, your spouse and yourself. No one, I repeat, *no one* would ever understand the complexity and the uniqueness of your marriage except the founder Himself – GOD, and the spouses involved. No matter what the case may be, as soon as you notice any abnormality in your marriage, get down on your knees and ask God for the wisdom and the grace to deal with it, while communicating the problem to your spouse. Do not wait for the situation to go from bad to worse, before you take it to God in prayer. In fact, whether there are immediate problems or not, there is always the need to ask God for the wisdom to make it through each day of our lives. Do not die in silence, however. If you feel the need or the urge to confide in someone, the need to let out the frustration, pain or suffering you are facing in your marriage, be sure to prayerfully pick the right person (preferably the closest family member to you) that could either join you in prayers or find other meaningful ways to help solve, and not compound, the problem.

Most importantly, even those who may have got it right still need to work at maintaining a beautiful, healthy and long lasting marriage. The difference between those who got it wrong and those who were led by God (those who got it right) lies in the fact that, while those who got it right might just be working only at maintaining a healthy marriage, those who got it wrong would have to first and foremost work at attaining a healthy marriage, before going to the next level of working at maintaining that healthy state of their marriage. As a wife, knowing your role in the home will go a long way in helping you build your home properly. (The next chapter of this book deals exhaustively with that.) In addition, the spouses involved in an unhealthy marriage must first be willing to make a change about the unhealthy state of their marriage. Secondly, they will need to surrender to God and trust Him completely to be able to heal their marriage wholly. Lastly, they should be ready to obey God's word on what a Christian marriage should look like, nothing more or less.

Every wife and mom must learn "contentment." Be contented with what you have, whatever that may be. Be contented with your own husband. In other words, accept your spouse regardless of whatever shortcomings he may have, because no one is perfect – only God is. A preacher once said: If only every woman would accept, love and cherish her own husband just as much as she accepts, loves and cherishes her own children; then so many marriages would begin to experience an extraordinary break through. Every woman should learn to see the bigger picture in her marriage. She should stop making comparisons and mind her own marriage because every marriage is unique. Marriage is not child's play. It takes constant maintenance by both spouses involved to make it a beautiful haven, regardless of any challenges experienced within that marriage. Remember, God has blessed every Christian union/marriage and a threefold cord– God, husband and wife – cannot easily be broken.

My final words to the young women out there: Since there is no place in the Bible that makes it okay for anyone to get divorced on any account whatsoever, I would strongly recommend that you look carefully before you leap. Do not be so much in a hurry to get married when certain important issues have not been settled in your spirit. It is often said that you cannot give what you do not have. In essence, every woman should have only greatness and nothing less, to offer.

Recommended tips to follow:

1. Give your life to God completely; no reservation whatsoever.

2. Endeavour to know His will for you and then, walk in it.

3. Make the right choices of friends. Don't just make friends! Make friends that will build you up and not tear you down.

4. Be involved in Godly activities and practices. In other words, flee ungodly practices and activities.

5. If you are old enough to be in a relationship, ensure that you do a lot of talking (good and effective communication), and greatly limit physical contact, in order to avoid any occasion of sin.

6. Abstain completely from *sex*. Flee (run away) from fornication. Anyone that has the spirit of God and is genuinely interested in you will *never* demand sex from you before marriage.

7. Go down on your knees and ask God for guidance in any relationship you are in. Ask God whatever you desire in your relationship and trust Him to lead you all the way.

8. Do your homework well by developing yourself spiritually, physically and otherwise (see chapter three of this book for guidance).

9. Having developed yourself, know what you want in a man and never settle for anything less than that. To buttress my point: There was a certain young woman who was in a relationship with a young man who smoked cigarettes and drank alcohol excessively. She found nothing wrong with those habits,

or maybe she did find something wrong with them, but thought they were probably a "man's thing" to drink and smoke. They eventually got married. For me on the other hand, I had an entirely different mind-set. I knew that those were bad habits and that there was everything wrong with them. I knew those habits could be a source of problems in any marriage. As such, I never wanted to enter into any relationship with any man with such habits. By the special grace of God, I got exactly what I wanted. I therefore urge you to pray for whatever you desire in a man and believe that it will be done for you as you desire. This leads me to my final point.

10. Renew your mind with the word of God on a daily basis. As you begin to experience fellowship with the word of God and get closer to Him, you will begin to have the mind of Christ. With time, the wisdom and

knowledge of God will guide you through all things pertaining to life.

A note of warning: Not every man or woman is marriageable. What I mean is this: If for instance a man beats up a woman he is in a relationship with, or vice versa; or, if for any reason either of the two parties in a relationship notices a bad habit other than physical abuse that could pose a threat in the marriage, do not be reluctant to put an end to that relationship, immediately. The only reason to go on with such a relationship is if the person in question with the bad habit is genuinely broken or repentant about that bad habit. The person has to be willing and committed to correcting that bad habit. Otherwise, there is no need to go on with such a dangerous relationship. Besides, only an encounter with God can genuinely change a person, no other person can. The story of Apostle Paul in the Holy Bible is a perfect example of what I am talking about. Apostle Paul (formerly called Saul) who once persecuted Christians was a completely changed man after his encounter with God on his way to Damascus **(Acts chapter 9)**.

A preacher once said; "If you decide to marry a stupid man, you should be prepared to be submissive to him." Do not be forced into a situation you would regret for the rest of your life. Do your homework properly and enjoy the rest of your life. A word they say is enough for the wise; and prevention is absolutely better than cure.

Having said all that, and having been led by God in your choice of a spouse, you should not stop there. Commit yourself to making your marriage work. Never ever treat your marriage with laxity or disdain. Even the right spouse may seem like the wrong one if we fail to do or put the right things in place.

2
A WOMAN'S ROLE AS A WIFE AND AS A MOM

From the perspective of acting, any role or character taken up by an actor has to be properly understood and the lines rehearsed in order to effectively portray that role or character. This also applies to the roles played by a couple. Thus, a role properly understood can be played out effectively.

We have now past beyond the issue of choosing the right spouse. A married woman is therefore obliged to know what her primary roles entail. One vital fact we often downplay or overlook is our role as a wife, as well as a mom. Many of us take it for granted; some are ignorant of it; while a few others are indifferent about it. How can we then be successful at what we know little or nothing about? Experiencing the beauty of motherhood and of being a wife does not happen overnight. There are certain facts we need to have at our finger tips and certain relevant discoveries we need to make about ourselves towards the achievement of this great feat. There is no doubt that being a wife and a mom together make for an amazing experience, but being truly successful at it makes it much more fulfilling and extremely rewarding.

Make no mistake about it; it was God who instituted marriage. Let us take a look at the corresponding books in the Bible **(GNB)**:

1. **Genesis 1:27: So God created human beings, making them to be like himself. He created them male and female.**

2. **Mathew 19:4-6: Jesus answered, "Haven't you read the scripture that says that in the beginning the Creator made people male and female? And God said, 'For this reason a man will leave his father and mother and unite with his wife,**

> and the two will become one.' So they are no longer two, but one. No human being must separate, then, what God has joined together."

3. **Genesis 2:24: That is why a man leaves his father and mother and is united with his wife; and they become one.**

It is therefore not out of place to categorically state that the only one who is fit/worthy to best define the role of any party within the institution of marriage is GOD, Our Creator, and as clearly stated above, the originator of marriage.

The reason why many wives/moms have problems in their marriages today is simply because they have decided to look outside the founder of this great institution. Sadly, many prospective and present wives/moms do not know what their duties/responsibilities in the home entail. Our society assumes that a wife/mom should naturally know and take up her responsibilities in the home. This is because it is assumed that every girl child was brought up by a mom (either biological or in the form of a guardian), and therefore should automatically be familiar with her responsibilities, and hence, be able to carry them out accordingly. But this is just not so in so many instances, and many marriages have crumbled due to this erroneous assumption. It is about time we started consciously nurturing our children the moment they become teenagers on the values of marriage, as well as their prospective roles in marriage. We must spell out their responsibilities according to what the Bible says, and not based on hearsay, or based on what we are familiar with that seems right. Parents and the religious bodies should particularly take up the responsibility of achieving this vital goal. This is very important in order to avoid unnecessary conflicts in marriages, and as much as possible, build more healthy homes in the near future.

In this chapter, we will get to understand and appreciate the roles of a wife and a mom based on the biblical perspective; GNB.

THE ROLE OF A WIFE

The role of a wife includes the following:

1. A wife is her husband's helper.

    It was God's idea to create a woman, not Adam's.

    > **Genesis 2:18: Then the LORD God said, "It is not good for the man to live alone. I will make a suitable companion to help him."**

    A woman was thus made to be a 'help' mate to her husband and not a 'spoiler' mate. A wife certainly has an obligation to help her husband achieve and not destroy his goals and aspirations.

2. A wife's body belongs to her husband.

1st Corinthians 7:3-5: A man should fulfill his duty as a husband, and a woman should fulfill her duty as a wife, and each should satisfy the other's needs. A wife is not the master of her own body, but her husband is; in the same way a husband is not the master of his own body, but his wife is. Do not deny yourselves to each other, unless you first agree to do so for a while in order to spend your time in prayer; but then resume normal marital relations. In this way you will be kept from giving in to Satan's temptation because of your lack of self-control.

In other words, do not deny each other of sexual pleasure. Give it to each other freely and unconditionally. Both husband and wife should feel extremely free with each other to discuss their sexual needs.

3. A wife is an Evangelist.

> **1st Peter 3:1-2: In the same way you wives must submit to your husbands, so that if any of them do not believe God's word, your conduct will win them over to believe. It will not be necessary for you to say a word, because they will see how pure and reverent your conduct is.**

A wife's conduct should lead her husband to God and not away from Him.

4. Submit to your husband as befits the Lord.

> **Colossians 3:18: Wives, submit to your husbands, for that is what you should do as Christians.**

> **Ephesians 5:22 & 24: Wives, submit to your husbands as to the Lord. And so wives must submit completely to their husbands just as the church submits itself to Christ.**

5. The husband is the head of the wife.

   > **Ephesians 5:23: For a husband has authority over his wife just as Christ has authority over the church; and Christ is himself the Saviour of the church, his body.**

6. A wife must respect her husband.

   > **Ephesians 5:33: But it also applies to you: every husband must love his wife as himself, and every wife must respect her husband.**

Wives have been commanded to respect their husbands. How hard could that possibly be? If you truly respect yourself enough, you would also have respect for the one that has been placed over you– *your husband!* Those who argue that a husband is not the head of his wife should be very careful what they say. Treat your spouse with utmost respect, whether you feel he deserves it or not. He is your covering; he has been placed over you by God. A good number of women who have lost their husbands would give anything to have them back. Sadly, those wives who still have theirs take them for granted. Stop grumbling and be very grateful to God for them. Never fail to treat them the way God expects you to. You may fall short sometimes, but never remain there. Repent of your sins, apologize for whatever wrong you may have committed, and retrace your footsteps back to the right path. Never ever feel too big to say you are sorry. I call "sorry" the magic word. It could melt the hardest of hearts if said sincerely. On the other hand, try not to slip so often that you render that magic word ineffective. Furthermore, being able to say "sorry" does not make you a weakling, as so many people erroneously believe. On the contrary, it makes you the bigger and more mature person. More so, it is to your spouse and not just anybody. I repeat: A husband is his wife's covering. God has placed him as the head over his wife. It is often said that the husband is the head while the wife is the neck, right? If that is the case, we all know that anatomically, in the human body, the head comes before the neck. The other way round no doubt, spells disaster. In fact, it could be referred to as a fatal case. No human being could possibly survive that sort of re-arrangement for obvious reasons. This logic can also be applied in the context of marriage. When a woman (referred to as the neck), tries to take up the role of her husband (referred to as the head), it never works out. In other words, it is always fatal. As a wife, if you give your husband the respect that is due to him, even if it may seem as though he does not deserve it, with time, he would definitely reciprocate. Even if he does not, you have your own part of the covenant to fulfill as a wife regardless of your husband's lack of fulfilling his own part. Let GOD be the judge and not you!

7. A wife's conduct should bring pride to her husband and not shame.

> **Proverbs 31:23: Her husband is well known, one of the leading citizens.**

THE EMBODIMENT OF A TRUE WOMAN

A woman's true beauty lies on the inside:

> **1st Peter 3:3 (AMP): Your adornment must not be merely external – with interweaving and elaborate knotting of the hair, and wearing gold jewellery, or dressing in expensive clothes.**

There is no doubt in the fact that a woman should look good at all times; but, not to the detriment of her inner being. Your character (the inner person) is who you really are. Your outward appearance and character should complement the inner person.

> **1st Peter 3:4 (AMP): But let it be the hidden person of the heart, with the imperishable quality and unfading charm of a gentle and**

peaceful spirit, which is very precious in the sight of God.

It should be worthy of note that the instructions given to wives in the Bible as regards their husbands are not conditional. Meaning, a wife has been instructed to love, respect, submit to her husband etcetera, completely; without attaching any form of conditions to any of the given instructions. **For instance; Ephesians 5:22 (GNB) says: "Wives, submit to your husbands as to the Lord."** Note that the instruction given was not for wives to submit to their husbands if their husbands love them. It says "submit," with no conditions attached. Thus, every wife is expected to carry out her responsibilities towards her husband regardless of what her husband does or how he treats her. Hence the Bible also says in **1st Peter 3:1 (GNB): "In the same way you wives must submit to your husbands, so that if any of them do not believe God's word, your conduct will win them over to believe. It will not be necessary to say a**

word."Again I say: let God be the Judge. God did not place a wife as judge over her husband, neither should a wife take up the role of the devil (who the Bible says is an accuser of the brethren); as seen in **Revelation 12:10 (AMP): "...For the accuser of our brothers and sisters has been thrown down, he who accuses them and keeps bringing charges against them before our God day and night."** Therefore, as a wife, your role towards your husband is the only role you have to play and nothing else. In essence, you do not have any obligation to be what you have not been called to be.

A character worthy of emulation by every woman can be seen in the book of Proverbs chapter 31, beginning from verse 10 of the Holy Bible. It showcases the qualities of a wife of noble character. The Bible describes her as a worthy, capable woman.

Verse 10: How hard it is to find a capable wife! She is worth far more than jewels!

Verse 11: Her husband puts his confidence in her, and he will never be poor.

Verse 12: As long as she lives, she does him good and never harm.

Verse 13: She keeps herself busy making wool and linen cloth.

Verse 16: She looks at land and buys it, and with money she has earned she plants a vineyard.

Verse 17: She is a hard worker, strong and industrious. (She is energetic and very hardworking)

Verse 22: She makes bedspreads and wears clothes of fine purple linen. (She takes good care of herself and looks good for her husband)

Verse 24: She makes clothes and belts, and sells them to merchants. (She is enterprising)

Verse 25: She is strong and respected and not afraid of the future.

Verse 30: Charm is deceptive and beauty disappears, but a woman who honours the LORD should be praised.

(All verses were taken from GNB)

THE ROLE OF A MOM

Again, Proverbs chapter 31 best describes this role.

1. She provides for her household.

   Verse 15 (GNB): She gets up before daylight to prepare food for her family and to tell her servant women what to do.

   Every mom should be able to provide good, healthy, tasty meals for her household, because it totally reflects on their overall wellbeing.

2. She is generous.

   Verse 20 (GNB): She is generous to the poor and needy.

3. She is prepared for eventualities.

Verse 21 (GNB): She does not worry when it snows, because her family has warm clothing.

4. She is wise.

   Verse 26 (GNB): She speaks with a gentle wisdom.

5. She is vigilant and never gives room to idleness.

   Verse 27 (GNB): She is always busy and looks after her family's needs.

In summary, Proverbs chapter 31, describes a virtuous woman. It describes her as a woman of wisdom, who is kind and responsible, who brings pride to her husband, is skillful, hardworking, industrious, is an entrepreneur, is not wasteful, who does not engage in idle talk, takes good care of herself and her household; and who extends her hands to the poor and needy as well.

What more can be said? In essence, she is well rounded. She is successful in her dealings both inside and outside her home. As a result of her conduct and overall success, verses 28-31 of that same chapter of the book of Proverbs (GNB), describe her rewards:

> **Her children show their appreciation, and her husband praises her. He says "many women are good wives but you are the best of them all". Give her credit for all she does. She deserves the respect of everyone.**

Be sure to diligently fulfill your roles as a wife and as a mom simultaneously, since both roles go hand in hand.

Further instructions and counselling as regards women can be seen in **Titus 2:3-5 (AMP):**

> **Older women similarly are to be reverent in their behaviour, not malicious gossips nor addicted to**

much wine, teaching what is right and good, so that they may encourage the young women to tenderly love their husbands and their children, to be sensible, pure, makers of a home, good-natured, being subject to their own husbands, so that the word of God will not be dishonoured.

As well as in:

1st Timothy 5:14 (AMP): So, I want younger widows to get married, have children, manage their households, and not give opponents of the faith any occasion for slander.

Becoming a woman of noble character is not farfetched. Every woman possesses the ability to become one; hence it is contained in the Holy Bible. As I had earlier mentioned under the role of a wife, it was God's idea to create woman, not Adam's. That means that becoming the woman you were created to be is indeed possible only by the special grace of God. God has deposited in every woman the ability to be successful both as a wife and a mom. Ask God for the grace and the strength to become the woman He has created you to be, while taking the necessary steps to ensuring that it be so, and watch how amazing your life will turn out.

Basically, for every mom out there, keeping your home together and seeing to its smooth operation should be your first and most important priority. Nothing in the world should take its place. Every other activity, profession, engagement or business deals should 'complement' and not lead to the 'neglect' of your home.

3
SELF-DISCOVERY AND DEVELOPMENT

Self-discovery is the unveiling of your inner being. It is a journey that must be embarked on in order to unravel your greatest potentials.

Getting to know yourself better would help to bring out the best in you. Until you get to understand yourself first and know more about your abilities, you cannot possibly attain your greatest heights. In addition to being a mom, every living being has something meaningful to contribute to the existence of humanity. Endeavour to discover your God-given purpose and begin fulfilling it before it is too late. In other words, every mom has an input to make both in the confines of her home, as well as in the world at large. Being able to balance every aspect of your life adequately is a key factor to being successful and finding lasting fulfillment.

I would strongly recommend for every prospective mom to get to know herself adequately in preparation to becoming a fulfilled mom. But, if you are already a mom, it is never too late to start this journey of self-discovery.

Stop for a moment and look within yourself. Ask yourself a few questions and try to provide answers to them. Feel free to jot down your answers for reference purposes. I will help you with some of the likely questions and hopefully you could attempt to answer them. Remember, there are no right or wrong answers. All you need to do is to be sincere with yourself. Here are some of the possible questions you could attempt to answer: How do you view the world at large? What positive impact can you as an individual make in the world? What are your abilities? What is the extent of your creativity and how can it be applied to problem solving? What drives you each day? What are you passionate about? What are your beliefs? What are your strengths and weaknesses? What are your likes and dislikes? What is your temperament? What are the likely things that could get you really upset? When you are upset, how do you cool off; and how long does it take you to achieve a state of calmness? How do you handle stress or stressful situations? What are your hobbies? What are your goals in life; and what steps are you currently taking to achieve those goals?

Do not limit yourself to the above questions. You could go on and on. Just bear in mind that it is all in an effort to help you get to know yourself better and not an avenue for self-condemnation. Take your time answering these questions. It could take you a few hours to a few days. It does not matter how long. What matters most is to achieve the objective of this exercise, which is self-discovery.

Having discovered so much about yourself and your abilities, the next step is 'self-development.' Generally speaking, self-development is encompassing. You could develop yourself:

1. **Spiritually:** Getting serious with one's spiritual life is a vital step to living a happy and fulfilled life. **Ecclesiastes 12:1 (AMP) says: "Remember also your Creator in the days of your youth, before the evil days come or the years near when you will say, "I have no enjoyment and delight in them."**

2. **Intellectually:** For those who may still be in school, it is important to acquire as much knowledge as you can in your area of study, as well as, a little or more in other areas of study. Getting serious with your studies in order to graduate with excellent grades is also very important. Do not acquire knowledge for the sake of it. Acquire knowledge with a purpose. Whatever knowledge you acquire at any point in your life

should upgrade and not downgrade you.

3. **Physically:** You have to gain proficiency in the act of looking good at all times. I am not saying that one should be extravagant about it. 'Good looks' starts from within. Eat right! Personal hygiene is also of utmost importance. Keep yourself and your environment neat and tidy at all times. The need to cultivate the habit of having good personal hygiene comes in very handy in marriage, especially when children come into the picture. You will not only be keeping yourself neat and tidy; you will also have to look after your spouse and children; that is no child's play. Only those who have gained proficiency in this can survive through the period without

breaking down or being thrown into a state of total mess and confusion. The fact is, if you are unable to take good care of yourself, you will definitely not be able to look after the ones you are to take care of or will be responsible for.

4. **Emotionally:** Learning how to put your emotions under your control is essential in self-development. Never, ever let your emotions get the better part of you. Master this and you will always be in control. More so, self-control is one of the fruits of the Holy Spirit: **Galatians 5:22-23 (AMP):**

> **But the fruit of the Spirit is love, joy, peace, patience, kindness, goodness,**

faithfulness, gentleness, self-control.

All you need to do is to ask God for it, and it will be yours.

5. Other relevant aspects of self-development include learning about:

   a. **Financial management:** You do not want to go bankrupt or live a life of borrowing. Learn to live within your means. Be content with what you have at all times.

   b. **Cooking skills:** Develop your cooking skills as much as you can. It is very important for a woman to be adept at this. Learn about healthy meals and how to prepare them. Apart from being fun, it is important in helping to maintain a healthy lifestyle and thus, a healthy family.

c. **Sporting activities:** If time permits, you may want to consider engaging in one or various sporting activities as a way of relaxation, physical development or just for the fun of it. Depending on your area or areas of interest, such activities include: swimming, table tennis, lawn tennis, basketball, and so on.

Specifically speaking, self-development involves building a positive character. **Character can be defined as all the qualities and features that make a person, groups of people, and places different from others (The Oxford Learner's Dictionary).** Positive character therefore, has to do with portraying good distinguishing features, qualities or characteristics. Every person is unique and has features that are particular only to that person, even in the case of identical twins. Each twin is created uniquely and for different purposes. The point is that you have been created for a specific purpose. Work at developing your God-given features or characteristics so that you will stand out of the crowd.

Let us see how we could possibly achieve this. First, I assume that you may have already completed the exercise given at the beginning of this chapter. Having done that, you may have discovered your strengths and weaknesses. Next, you have to work on developing both your strengths and your weaknesses. You may ask, "How?" Well, your strengths are your strongest points or your areas of expertise. What great skills do you have? They could either be innate or acquired. How can you improve on those skills, or on the knowledge you may have gained in a particular field of study?

On the other hand, your weaknesses are inadequate qualities or faults that you possess. How can you improve on these inadequacies? How can you turn your weaknesses into strengths? After you have discovered and admitted that you have weaknesses, you need to be willing to make a change. Look for ways to improve on these faults or inadequacies. Get some help from professionals if the need arises.

Again, it is not just enough to develop yourself and stop there. We have what we call empowerment. Empowerment affords us the opportunity to give back to humanity what we have gained in any way possible. I believe at this point, you may have already found ways to improve on your strengths. Now, you will need to ask yourself some pertinent questions that will empower you. Questions such as: how can this skill (whether innate or acquired) or knowledge be of benefit to me, as well as others around me; of what use is it? Put in other words, how can I be useful to myself and those around me? How can I positively change or affect lives around me? In what possible ways can I give back to humanity what I have acquired? However the questions appear, they should be able to help you take what you are or have to offer to an entirely different level. There has to be willingness and commitment on your part to give back. That is, you have to consciously cultivate the habit of wanting to give back the knowledge, expertise or resources you have acquired. Nothing is gained by holding back what you have to offer. Give freely because whatever knowledge you have, was made possible by God. One way to give back would be to become a mentor. By so doing we are able to produce better individuals to whom we can pass the baton. Better individuals leads to a better society, and hence a better tomorrow.

The long and short of it is that you have to look for possible ways to bring your knowledge or expertise to good use. Do not allow it to remain dormant in you. Let others around you benefit from it. Basically, do not be selfish with whatever knowledge or skill you might have acquired as a person. Let your presence and your impact be felt in the community, society and the world at large.

Mathew 5:14-16 (AMP): "You are the light of the world. A city set on a hill cannot be hidden; nor does anyone light a lamp and put it under a basket, but on a lamp stand, and it gives light to all who are in the house. Let your light shine before men in such a way that they may see your good deeds and moral excellence, and glorify your Father who is in heaven."

4

NURTURE YOUR CHILDREN WITH A SENSE OF PURPOSE

A building that stands the test of time is always built on a solid foundation. Hence the foundation of a child in every stage of development is of utmost importance. When the foundation is faulty, the entire building collapses in no time.

"We are guilty of many errors and many faults, but our worst crime is abandoning the children, neglecting the fountain of life. Many of the things we need can wait. The child cannot. Right now is the time his bones are being formed; his blood is being made; and his senses are being developed. To him we cannot answer 'tomorrow,' his name is today" (Gabriela Mistral). The rate of growth and development within the first year of a child's life is incredible. A child who initially lacks neck control, is unable to sit, crawl, walk or run, is able to achieve all of the above within just a year of being born (for most children). There is no time to waste in the nurturing of a child once a child is born. Several things we need, desire or intend to do can wait. On the other hand, the nurturing of a child cannot be postponed or put on a waiting list. It is either *now* or *never*!

Nurturing your children and getting to know them is the main objective of motherhood. It is not just about raising a child, animals do only that. Nurturing a child involves conscious effort. In essence, we should be very mindful of our way of life and the principles we imbue in our children. We moms should be our children's first role model. We should lead by example because children do what you do and also say what you say. Keep in mind that getting to know your children is a continuous process which must be done diligently and with much patience. It is important to note that every child is unique; wisdom is therefore required when nurturing children.

They say there is no place like home. There is none indeed! The home must be a safe haven for children to run to, especially in difficult times. Children must feel a sense of belonging and security in the home. Endeavour to create a peaceful atmosphere in the home.

A lot goes into nurturing one's children: giving them tender care, nursing or nourishing, training and educating them. Tender care is a fond, loving, gentle and sweet way of caring for someone. For a better understanding, I will give the meaning (taken from the Oxford Learner's Dictionary) of the individual words, as used in the above definition.

Fond: Feeling affection for somebody; affectionate

Loving: Feeling or showing love and affection for somebody; affectionate

Gentle: Calm and kind; doing things in a quiet and careful way.

Sweet: Having or showing a kind character.

Clearly, tender care is about having an affectionate, kindly and pleasing disposition towards one's children.

Nursing and/or nourishing a child involves caring for and helping a person to grow and be healthy. It has to do with bringing up, rearing, helping to grow, fostering or the like. In nursing or nourishing a child, a mom is expected to breast feed or give the required nourishment to help that child grow and develop as expected. Training children generally involves guiding them through their childhood. It involves bringing them up to have good social skills, imparting in them values, principles and the rules of living that will guide them throughout their lifetime. **Proverbs 22:6 (AMP) says: "Train up a child in the way he should go; even when he is**

old he will not depart from it." In essence, as a mom, we should not just raise our children for the sake of it. We should do it consciously, with a sense of purpose.

On the other hand, educating children has to do with teaching them, giving them the necessary instructions about life in general; from their way of life; to the acquisition of knowledge that will help them excel both in their academics and in everything they set out to accomplish in life; to the development of their innate abilities and a lot more. That means, the mom is the first teacher of a child, and the home is the first actual classroom of a child.

The pertinent question is: As a Parent, what are you doing presently to help your children in their developmental process? What morals or values are you instilling in your children? What are your set goals towards raising them? What strategic plans do you have towards their future? What sort of habits are you instilling in them?

That reminds me. It is very sad to note that quite a number of moms have neglected the aspect of keeping themselves, their children and their surroundings neat and tidy. The effect of this sort of neglect would invariably rub off on one's children in the long run. It is very important for every mom to teach her children the relevance of good personal hygiene, as well as, living in a neat and tidy environment at all times. More importantly, it is not just about saying it; it has to start with you doing it! Actions they say, speak louder than words. God bless my mom! My siblings and I can attest to being raised by a mom with a very high standard of personal hygiene. It has definitely rubbed off on us in a very good way. Today, keeping ourselves and our environment neat and tidy has become a habit (a very good one at that!). It has become a way of life for us. She did not only tell us what to do and how to go about it, she led by example. Good personal hygiene can be developed at any stage in one's life. It just takes a little commitment, and above all, the willingness to want to change your current situation. Some people may argue that "habits die hard," but remember; nothing is impossible to a willing heart. Ask God for the grace and strength to effect whatever change in your life you intend to make. Children learn faster by what they see or hear you say than what you tell them or have them do. As such, the conditions in which you raise your children will engender in them either being neat and tidy individuals or dirty and untidy (unkempt) individuals. The choice is yours. However, endeavour to make the right choices for the sake of your children's overall well-being and state of mind; the reason being that, the prevailing conditions in which we raise our children, generally, affect them either positively or negatively. It certainly takes a lot of effort to be neat and tidy, but it definitely pays off in the long run. On the other hand, being lazy, dirty and untidy never pays off.

As a mother, being the one closer to your children than their father or any other member of the family (most times), puts you at an advantage in being able to effectively relate with them. You should never get tired of listening attentively to everything they have to say, even if it may seem as though they are not making any sense. As a mom you should be able to communicate effectively with your children. Try to relate to their feelings as much as possible, and at all times. This will help you discover a lot about them and assist you in guiding them properly. Every mom should help her children utilize their God-given potential to full capacity amidst the growing challenges we face in the world today. Help them discover and develop their talents in the best possible ways. Having done your best in raising your children, stop complaining or getting worried and try to enjoy and cherish every moment you spend with them. Since every moment comes with its particularities, choose to learn from each moment and do away with uncertainties and regrets because you are only sure of that present moment; you do not know what tomorrow may bring.

Moreover, before long, your children will become adults. Having graduated from school, they will leave home to get jobs and be married, and they will eventually raise children of their own. We should work towards cultivating good principles and habits in them; and much more, we must strive to leave a lasting legacy in their lives, enough to see them through a lifetime, and also to pass on the baton to their own children.

Every mom is expected to also look out for her children beyond their childhood, that is, up to adulthood. Be vigilant and prepared to protect their interest in a positive manner. Please do not get me wrong. I am not advocating that you dictate or impose your desires or interests on your children. Neither do I advocate that you impose a spouse of your choice on them. Let me give you an insight into what I mean.

At the age of eighteen, a child is considered an adult (fully grown person) in most parts of the world, and should be left to make his or her own decisions and also be ready to face the consequences of any action or decision taken. If you may have noticed, the active role of a mom (a parent) in the life of a child is usually from infancy to about fourteen years of age or a little less than that. This duration of time in the life of a child is referred to as the formative years of that child. This period is the ultimate period to make a lasting impression on any child. Beyond age fourteen, a child begins to have a mind of his own and wants to be left alone to make decisions. Therefore, if a mom (or a parent) fails to nurture her child correctly during that period (infancy to age 14), then she could as well forget about it. It is only by a divine intervention that one could achieve it beyond age fourteen. I am quite sure that no one wants to rely upon a divine intervention to get it right. Besides, prevention they say is better than cure.

To better illustrate my point, there is a saying which goes like this: It is only a young plant with a green succulent stem and great flexibility that can be bent to any desired position without being broken. But, when the stem of a plant is old, dry and has lost its flexibility, it can no longer be bent as desired. Any attempt to forcefully bend the plant at that stage will invariably cause it to break. Basically, we only have a set period of time in the lives of our children to get it right at nurturing them appropriately, so that we could get the best out of them in future. The formative years of a child are very crucial. It is what you put into that child in the formative years that you would likely get out of that child in his or her later years (adulthood). It follows the principle of GIGO (Garbage In, Garbage Out) in Computer Science. GIGO is a Computer Science acronym that implies bad input will result in bad output. In other words, you cannot get a bean plant from planting a maize seed. It is against nature. Hence the saying: you cannot give what you do not have.

Some people may argue that even when a parent does his or her best in nurturing a child in the right way, a few may sometimes still go astray. For the purpose of emphasis, I will quote again **Proverbs 22:6 (AMP), which says: "Train up a child in the way he should go; even when he is old he will not depart from it."** That is God's word and it is the *truth*. Parents are the ones with the sole responsibility of training their children. Not the teachers in the school, or the Sunday school teachers, or any other person. Be responsible for your own child and stop shifting your responsibilities to others. I am not ignoring the role of peer groups, the television, the internet and many other factors that influence a child during the formative years. The fact is, even when a child that has been properly nurtured goes astray, there is a higher chance of that child retracing his/her footsteps back to where he/she missed it.

It takes a village to raise a child, some people say. Notwithstanding, parents have the greatest influence on a child and are usually blamed for a badly brought up child than any other being or entity. If you are in disagreement, why is it that when a child turns out badly, character wise, the blame always goes to the parents or the guardian of that child? Why is it that the accusing fingers are never pointed at others like the teachers, the society or someone else other than the parents or guardians of that badly brought up child? Parents should not shy away from their responsibilities. Forget about external influences and play your own part to the best of your ability. Live up to your responsibilities before it is too late. Chastise your children while you still can, so that they will not have to chastise you during your old age. A word, they say, is enough for the wise.

Ideally, the burden of parenting should be shared between both parents. But, in reality, most of the responsibilities are shouldered by the mothers. Fathers are most times too busy looking out for ways to provide for their families, and as such have little or no time to spend with their children.

Therefore, mothers are forced to nurture the children for the most part.

Recall what I said earlier about looking out for your children. Beyond the formative years, the role of a mom (or parent) towards her children becomes more limited and passive as the years go by. Hence, beyond the formative years, a mom (or a parent) then takes up the role of a counsellor/adviser (being more experienced and having seen more of life, one should be better equipped to offer useful advice when the need arises), a spiritual intercessor and a support for her children in times of need. It could go beyond the aforementioned as the case may be. By taking up these more passive roles, you could as well be said to be looking out for your children and helping to protect their interests positively. The fact is, if you have done your homework well in the area of nurturing your children, you should be able to confidently and comfortably stay backstage when they eventually become adults. What I mean is that you should be able to sit back, relax, take up the passive roles and trust God to see them through their adulthood and, indeed, their lifetime.

Most importantly, parents should never neglect the spiritual life of a child. The spiritual life of a child needs to be nurtured and encouraged to blossom fully. You could start by teaching the child how to say the grace before and after meals. A child should be taught how to kneel down to pray before going to bed and on waking up in the morning. They should be taught to know Him the only true GOD and JESUS CHRIST whom He sent to save mankind. Knowing GOD, trusting Him and believing in Him is the very essence of life. Like I mentioned earlier, it is very dangerous to be outside of God's will for your life. In other words, do not fail to teach your children that very vital part of life, their spirituality.

To the Christian moms out there, I urge you to pray ceaselessly for your children, while raising them in the fear of God. Never get tired of praying.

Prophesy into their lives as often as possible and watch what God will make out of them.

5

SET YOUR PRIORITIES RIGHT

Our priorities are a reflection of who we are and what we represent.

In setting your priorities right, remember that you were first a wife before becoming a mom. Hence, in performing your motherly duties, you must also perform your wifely duties at the same time. Both roles go hand in hand. It is possible to enjoy, as well as, excel in carrying out both roles, if only you are able to set your priorities right.

I cannot help but talk about my observation in recent times. Social media is fast taking over a significant proportion of our time, and so many moms have become victims of it. Social media should be used to your advantage and not your detriment. It is okay to be on social media only when it is absolutely necessary to do so. However, it should not prevent you from carrying out your responsibilities in the home; neither should it render you completely unproductive or simply a mere nuisance. Stop for a moment and examine yourself. How many hours of the day do you spend on unproductive activities, such as watching non-educative programs, tweeting, glancing through Facebook profiles and other unnecessary applications, playing games, snooping around on others, idle talk? The list is endless. Those wasteful hours may span from a few minutes in a day to a few hours in a day, to a few days in a week, to a few weeks in a month, to a few months in a year and then, to a few years in your lifetime. Is it really worth it? Remember, those wasted hours can never be retrieved. It indeed baffles me. Come to think of it, there are a billion and one useful things to be done each day. There are so many personal assignments left undone. It seems as though we have plenty of time in our hands to while away. It is about time you chose wisely and quickly how to turn those unproductive hours into productive ones because you can never turn back the hands of time. As a wife and a mom, you have naturally become the pivot of your home. The onus lies on you to make appropriate decisions, and in good time. Your goal should always be to take your family to the next level of greatness; of course, while also walking in agreement with your spouse.

Now that you have decided to set your priorities right, hopefully, you will have to learn to discover what works for you and what does not. Knowing what works for you can only be discovered over time. As you go about your daily activities, you will begin to discover what works for you and what does not. Take note of the things that work for you and incorporate them into your schedule, and make sure to do away with the things that do not work for you.

The worse thing that any mom can do to herself is to make comparisons. Mrs. A does this activity well;

therefore, I should be able to do it as well. You do not live in the same house as Mrs. A to know how she is able to achieve whatever she does so well. Mrs. B is so good at that chore, so I should be able to do it better. Instead of making comparisons or trying to outdo anyone, discover what you are good at and use it to your advantage. Everyone is good at something. Your concern should be to discover yours and make it work for you. Make sure you do away with jealousy, envy and strife because they only end up affecting you negatively.

Make daily plans that are realistic. Remember, there is no end to chores. Therefore, keep it as simple and as practical as possible. Know when to draw the line and call it a day. If you have grown up children, ensure that you assign some chores to them. It helps them become hardworking and responsible individuals. They say "an idle mind is the devil's workshop." Interestingly, children are usually very eager to work. They love being busy. Be creative about assigning chores. Make it fun. However, you should know the limits of every child and do not overdo it.

It is advisable to always have a to-do-list or a checklist which acts as a memory aid. This could be a list containing your daily, weekly, monthly or yearly activities. This is very helpful in order to avoid leaving out activities or completely missing out on important events or activities. A more advanced checklist would be a schedule that helps you remember tasks according to the time of day or other prevailing factors, thereby helping you prioritize and organize your activities within a given space of time. Basically, be very practical and keep it as simple and achievable as possible.

The bottom line is that as a mom, you should learn to set your priorities right at all times and also take out time to discover what works for you and stick to it. However, you could decide to make necessary adjustments to whatever works for you with time, if the need arises. Most importantly, whatever changes you make along the way must work to your advantage and not your disadvantage.

6

TAKE A BREAK

A reasonable time off work or any other routine activity is all we need to rejuvenate and remain sane.

Genesis 2:2(AMP) says: "And by the seventh day God completed His work which He had done, and He rested on the seventh day from all His work which he had done." Even God, our Creator, rested from all His work. Awesome!

Our bodies need some rest from time to time. Having accomplished your tasks for the day, you should take a break. It is extremely important to take a break to cool off whenever you can. This helps to calm your nerves and revitalize your body to be able to take on future tasks. You definitely would not want to get out of control and start yelling, and getting angry at everyone around you at the slightest provocation, otherwise known as "transferred aggression".

Some people may cool off by spending time with family. It may be in the form of vacations. Days could be specifically set aside for family time – every weekend, once a month and so on as the case may be. Figure out what schedule works well for you and stick to it. Remember, the focus or goal is about taking a break to cool off. Avoid any instance or instances that would increase your stress load.

If you have successfully carried out the exercise proposed in chapter three of this book, you might have identified a few ways on how to handle stress or stressful situations. Most importantly, you should endeavour to ease stress in a healthy way. Do not eat or over indulge in junk food, all in a bid to ease stress. Eat right! Eating the right meals helps boost your energy levels tremendously, as well as your immune system, thereby reducing the frequency of tiredness and also significantly reducing the likelihood of suffering from various ailments.

They say health is wealth. Good health should and must be our priority. Without good health, we cannot achieve very much in life. Some illnesses may even put a stop to one's career or even one's entire life.

A valid point we moms must never forget or take for granted is keeping fit. Let us endeavour to always keep fit both on the inside and on the outside. The combination of eating right and engaging in regular fitness exercises helps you achieve the aim of keeping fit both on the inside as well as on the outside. You do not necessarily have to go to a fitness centre or a gym in order to achieve this. Everything boils down to discipline. You could get DVDs on fitness exercises. If it is possible to obtain one, two or a few pieces of fitness equipment, then go ahead and do just that. Like I always say, "Know what works for you and stick to it." No matter what stage you are in your life presently, it is never too late to adopt a change of lifestyle. Do not wait until you fall ill as a result of certain bad habits you may be practising currently. Make a change and effect that change right now!

Basically, you have to stay healthy as much as you can, so as to be around long and healthy enough to spend a lifetime with your spouse, watch and help your children grow and become successful individuals, and also to contribute your own quota to the existence of humanity.

7

CAREER AND PARENTING

Parenting; a job that neither gets the attention nor the credit it deserves. The quality of children being raised today is a reflection of our tomorrow.

Children should never be left to raise themselves under the guise of survival of the fittest. Many children nowadays lack moral values; they behave irresponsibly, live recklessly and have no respect for elders. The incidence of teenage pregnancy is on the increase, drug abuse by teenagers is not left out. The list of vices exhibited by badly brought up children is endless. Having a successful career is very commendable. However, it should not be achieved at the expense of raising one's children. As I mentioned earlier, the responsibility of raising one's children ought to be shared equally by both parents. In reality, however, the mom takes the lion's share. Still, that should not be an excuse for neglecting the responsibility of raising and nurturing one's children.

Sadly, nowadays, many moms are unable to have a career and meet the demands of motherhood simultaneously without one of the two having to suffer. The choice of many women to become house wives in recent times may not necessarily be because of their spouse's decision for them to stay back; which may however be the case of a select few. Rather, it stems from the necessity to personally raise their children into becoming well-grounded individuals in a world full of so many controversies and contradictions.

The utmost responsibility of raising children these days is no joke. Back in the days, especially in Nigeria where I grew up, several moms benefited from the help of relatives, and in some instances, non-relatives as well, for assistance. Mothers were able to go about their careers and their various businesses as the case may be, without having to worry so much about the home front. These days, the case is different. Times have changed. People are aligning with the changing times. Individuals seem to be less honest and less trustworthy than in the past.

In my case, I am extremely deliberate in raising my children. I teach them all the time and virtually everywhere. I do it at the slightest opportunity I have – in the kitchen, while giving them a bath, in their bedrooms, in the living room, during play time and so on. We are in constant communication. I teach them about every subject. Most importantly, I teach them about God, using stories from the Holy Bible (their favourite time ever).

As for my career, I have never been someone who settles for less. I do everything to the best of my ability. I did not want to get just any job or do just anything for the sake of it. I wanted to do something that I was passionate about and enjoyed doing.

Sometimes, as a mom, your dream career may be impossible to achieve due to certain prevailing circumstances. Adapting to that circumstance may be by - taking up a more convenient career path for the good of the family; especially the children who may eventually become the victims of a bad choice. My daughter once complained about not being able to chew with the left side of her mouth as a result of an erupting tooth. She was just about five years old. I responded by telling her to refrain from chewing with that side of her mouth for the time being, which meant that she would have to learn to chew with only the right side of her mouth. It later dawned on me that the situation my daughter was going through could be likened to the challenges we face in life generally, as well as in motherhood. It was my daughter's first actual life lesson–*adaptation* (a special quality of human beings). My exact point: learn to adapt to any situation you cannot change. Some situations are only temporary, as in the case of my daughter. Others may be permanent. As a mother, we may not be able to change some of the challenges we face in motherhood, hence the need for adaptation.

Sacrifices are not very easy to make. By the grace of God, I decided to stay back home to personally raise my children – one of the best decisions of my life. I am challenging women all over the world to partake in the upbringing of their children. Do not just raise children; nurture them with a sense of purpose.

For a long time I battled within myself on how to juggle my family and my career. I had been home for a couple of years nurturing the children while my husband worked. My children had become a huge part of my life, and the quality of their upbringing, education and overall wellbeing mattered more to me than anything else in the world. I cared more about their success and progress in life than mine. Turning back the hands of time, I never imagined myself as a full time house wife. I had always wanted to work. Not just working, but working diligently to earn a living. I never thought for once I would be financially dependent on my husband. Here I was, many years down the line, being everything I never imagined I would become. Do not get me wrong. I have no regrets whatsoever. I love my life. I have a sweet husband with a beautiful heart and wonderful, adorable children, whom I love so much and hold very dear to my heart. That was all I had ever hoped for. Yet, inside I felt dissatisfied. Even though I laboured everyday for the wellbeing of my family and was overseeing most of the responsibilities of raising and nurturing the children, I felt idle. Yes! Idle in the sense that I was redundant in the workforce. I was unemployed and had no business at hand. I was criticized by concerned family members and friends. That was their way of looking out for me. I appreciate that! Unknown to them, for the first time in my life it was difficult for me to decide on what to do for the time being while raising and nurturing my children. I knew I would have to go back to work at some point. But, I needed to have something to do in the interim. Every career path I would have loved to take seemed to get in the way of raising my children the way I had planned to. I was not trying to give excuses for not going back to work. In fact, laziness is not a part of my personality. Being a workaholic and a very dedicated person, I feared that I would neglect my responsibilities as a mother in the process of trying to earn a living. Moreover, I did not want my children to be at the mercy of a total stranger; if I had to hire a nanny to look after them while I was away at work. I wondered and still wonder how parents are able to abdicate their responsibilities in raising and nurturing their children without feeling any sense of guilt. Some may argue that they cannot afford not to have jobs as a result of the financial shortfall of their spouses. Well understood! While not trying to sound insensitive, I still insist that moms should take up more flexible jobs for the sake of their children. You could take up temporary jobs that would ensure that your children are raised by you and not someone incapable of or completely inexperienced in doing the job of parenting. Money is good and valuable, but moulding your children into becoming honorable individuals is of greater value. In essence, be careful not to swap the essential for the nonessential.

That brings me to sacrifice. As moms, we should realize the need to make sacrifices for the smooth running of the home. Ideally, both parents should make sacrifices. Sadly, this is not always the case. A man is wired differently from a woman. Both have different roles and responsibilities to play as well. As for a husband, God has placed him head of his wife. **Ephesians 5:23 (AMP): For the husband is head of the wife, as Christ is head of the Church, Himself being the Saviour of the body.** Have you ever wondered why a man works so hard to provide for his household? **1st Timothy 5:8(AMP): If**

anyone fails to provide for his own, and especially for those of his own family, he has denied the faith and is worse than an unbeliever. In most cases, there is a greater pressure on a man to provide for his family than on a woman. A man goes all out to achieve success in his career at all cost, even to the detriment of his family sometimes. Almost, and in some cases in fact, leaving the responsibility of raising the children entirely to their wives. Moms are then forced to take the bull by the horn, which is a much smarter choice than abandoning the children to themselves or to total strangers in the name of nannies. The fact remains that if any child is hurt or deformed as a result of negligence, the mom is the one who suffers the consequences the most. Think about it!

Abdicating one's responsibilities as a parent is never the best option. Mothers! Wake up! The care giver/domestic worker cleans the house, prepares the meals, bathes the children, feeds them and puts them to bed. What then is your role as a mother to that child? Many care givers are very unreliable. Sometimes they have ulterior motives. Some others carry out their responsibilities grudgingly. The latter are usually very unhappy and uncaring towards the children being catered for. In the long run, these children are maltreated and abused, physically, sexually and emotionally. Eventually, they become disoriented. The psychological impact on these children cannot be ignored. They grow up into angry, resentful, uncaring and unstable individuals, among other problems that may become evident in later years. Only a handful of these care givers are reliable. How can one possibly tell the difference by mere physical appearance alone? Why take chances at the expense of your children? Aside from the maltreatment received by these children from their care givers; let us not forget about the inexperience of such individuals with regards to parenting. No one can look after your children better than or as well as yourself.

The craze for wealth and other material possessions is fast becoming a driving force operating in the minds of many individuals these days. Most people want to get rich quickly without engaging in any useful or legal activity. They engage in all sorts of crime to get rich. This probably may be one of the reasons why many individuals can no longer be relied upon. This change in the behavioural pattern of many individuals has forced a good number of mothers to forfeit their career, or in some cases, take time off to raise their children before going back to their careers rather than employing the likes of these individuals for assistance in the home. Some of these moms would rather engage in businesses that would afford them ample time for their children while carrying out their businesses.

Growing up for me was awesome. I would be extremely glad to have a replay of my childhood experiences. My siblings and I grew up with very strong family values. We took our spiritual lives seriously. I loved and still love the things of God. In my candid opinion, my parents did a fantastic job at nurturing my siblings and me. They are indeed the best! Though not flawless, it only goes to show that they are human beings and not GOD. Overall, I would give them an "A." As a result of my strong Godly and family values, I could not easily be swayed or influenced by peer groups. As a teenager, it was in fact impossible to sweep me off my feet. I was well grounded in almost every area. I was very sound, spiritually, academically, emotionally and otherwise. Our parents never failed to meet our needs; our wants were treated differently. For the sake of clarity, needs are necessities that you cannot do without. Wants on the other hand, are things that you desire but can be done without. As a result of the satisfaction and love I got from home, no one could lure me into any form of unholy relationships for material gains. The show of love from my parents was enough for me. This goes to show that the love of a parent towards a child cannot and should never be replaced.

Wondering why I am laying so much emphasis on raising and nurturing children the right way? Children are our future. The quality of the children we raise today determines the quality of our tomorrow. As parents, we have a huge task ahead of us. Do not leave your children to chance, be deliberate in raising them.

There is no hard and fast rule to being successful both in your career as well as in the management of your home. Ultimately, it is a case of having checks and balances. Know what works for you and stick to it. The most important thing for moms is to make decisions that will benefit everyone in the home. I do not think that any member of your family has to suffer for any of your decisions. It may be difficult to arrive at decisions that would benefit every member of the family equally, but it is achievable. Again, I quote **Proverbs 14:1 (GNB), which says: "Homes are made by the wisdom of women, but are destroyed by foolishness."** Be the best career mom you could possibly be. For moms with good family support, take advantage of that because with a very good family support, that is, for those with reliable close family members that could render very useful assistance at home, it is much easier to achieve success as a career mom.

By and large, in order to avoid unnecessary conflicts in marriage regarding career and responsibilities in the home, couples would do well to cover the issue before deciding to tie the knot.

8

A CHEATING SPOUSE

The fear of the LORD is the beginning of wisdom-Proverbs 9:10;

Psalm 111:10

Marriage is not a bed of roses. Rather, it could be likened to an institution of learning where no one knows it all. It must and should involve the coming together of two mature minds willing to tolerate each other's shortcomings.

I am going to deal strictly with cheating only within the confines of marriage. Without any doubt, cheating on a spouse is *adultery*. No matter the form in which it presents itself, whether by way of flirting with, conceiving the idea of sleeping with or being involved in the actual act of sleeping with anyone other than your spouse, it is adultery. Why should adultery be an option for an ailing spouse?

There is no justifiable reason whatsoever to commit adultery.

There have been various misconceptions about why men or women cheat on their spouses. Most times, the men and women involved in such acts of promiscuity do not fully understand the actual reason for their involvement in such shameful acts; even though they claim to know. They try to give various reasons to justify their actions in order to convince and also confuse people about their involvement in the act of promiscuity.

I love the story of Joseph in the Holy Bible. The book of Genesis chapter 39 gives details about how Joseph fled from the sin of fornication. In this instance, Joseph was not married; on the other hand, Potiphar's wife was. Potiphar's wife was bent on committing adultery with Joseph. The story tells us about how well-built and handsome Joseph was; and how Potiphar's wife took notice of him. She tried to lure him to bed, but Joseph refused to succumb. **In Genesis 39:9 (KJV), Joseph says: "There is none greater in this house than I; neither hath he kept back anything from me but thee, because thou art his wife: how then can I do this great wickedness, and sin against God?"** Obviously, Joseph had respect for his master, but most importantly; he feared God. That is my point! A man or a woman who fears God will never ever cheat on the spouse. I will restrict myself to men who cheat, for the purpose of educating moms.

Men who cheat do not necessarily do it because of their spouse's shortcomings. I only wish men could be more honest about the reasons why they cheat rather than just cooking up stories. A man cheats most times because he has conceived in his heart that it is okay to cheat. Some even say that it is a man's world. They see absolutely nothing wrong with it. Over time, it becomes a bad habit difficult to overcome. A few of them just do not care about the feelings of their spouses (they could be described as nonchalant). For them, anything goes.

On the other hand, there are some men who have made up their minds never to cheat on their spouses, no matter what happens in their homes or what shortcomings their spouses may have. Many of these men who have decided to stay faithful to their wives do so for various reasons; some of these men have the fear of God in them. Having studied the word of God, these men have gained enough wisdom that enables them to restrain themselves from such sinful acts in order not to incur the wrath of God. Others, who do not necessarily have the fear of God, dread the diseases associated with promiscuity, which is just enough to keep them at bay. Yet, a tiny proportion of those who do not cheat do so to avoid damaging their image. They do not want their names being dragged through the mud or the possible disgrace they may have to face when such shameful acts are exposed through the pregnancy of the other woman or through any other means.

I have heard and seen men who give various kinds of flimsy excuses for engaging in such acts. I once had a conversation with one such man. He likened his wife to a pot of soup (how callous!). He said he would love to taste other types (that is, to have side chicks), other than the pot of soup he had at home (his wife). Others claim that their wives do not take good care of themselves – they have become too fat and unattractive, and even look unkempt most times. A good number complain that their wives have little or no time for them. They complain that their wives spend most of their time attending to the needs of the children and have completely neglected their duties towards them.

Wives...listen up! Most men will never understand how tedious the role of a mom can be and may never get to appreciate the bulk of responsibilities a mom has to shoulder each day. The few that may fully understand are those that have actually worn the shoes of their wives at some point. That is, those that have had to take over the responsibilities of their wives in the home, due to certain circumstances such as certain forms of ailment; or as a result of their wives' complete absence from the home. A lack of understanding on the part of most husbands leads to a lack of appreciation of their wives. Due to that fact it is your responsibility as a wife to communicate these concerns to your husband and find ways to strike a balance between your wifely and motherly duties. Remember, you were a wife first, before you became a mom. You cannot and should not neglect your wifely duties. Find ways to work out your schedule and resolve your issues without compounding them. Chapter five of this book will help you gain some insight on how to go about it.

The right partner is the first step in the right direction. Couples should marry for the right reasons (see chapter one of this book). A man is the head of his home. If a man truly marries his wife out of pure love for her, he should allow that same love guide him whenever he needs to solve whatever problems encountered in his marriage. Men please, get in here! The reality is that moms are almost always weighed down by the numerous responsibilities they have to face in the home. So many women have lost their identities as a result of that. A husband can afford not to lift a pin in the home and get away with it; but a wife cannot afford that. Everything would go wrong if she decides to neglect her duties. There would be complete chaos in that home. Due to that fact, a wife works round the clock. She bears in mind that she cannot be seen as a failure. She breaks her back for the smooth running of the home. I am not trying to give excuses for moms. It is a fact that must be told. Every husband should be able to communicate effectively with his wife to know what challenges she is facing in the home and find ways to help her. Most especially, a husband should appreciate his wife for her efforts in the home. A husband should be his wife's support and shield. Do not bring her down in the presence of family members or even friends, colleagues or co-workers. Remember, you chose her – deal with it!

Back to wives! I implore you to make some effort to effect a change when the need arises. Do not give up on your marriage. Having seen the major reasons why men cheat and the excuses given by some of these men, the ball is in your court. It is now left for you to play your part. Do not give your spouse any room for excuses. Try not to neglect your wifely or motherly duties. Do not abdicate your sole responsibilities. There are some responsibilities that could be abdicated, and there are others that cannot. It is your job to figure that out. Take good care of yourself, your spouse, the children and the home. Spice up your marriage. Try out new but safe ways to go about it. Be adventurous, not rigid and boring. Of course, with the grace of God, you can achieve all your set goals.

Above everything, pray at all times. **1st Thessalonians 5:17: Pray without ceasing.** What I mean is this, get down on your knees and pray for your spouse, yourself and your children. Study the word of God. Remember, the fear of God is the beginning of wisdom. Wisdom is needed to achieve success in every area of one's life. The fear of God is what is needed to keep a spouse from cheating. Not your beauty, or the beautiful dresses and night gowns or the jewellery that you wear. Not even the sumptuous meals you prepare would keep him from cheating on you if he does not fear God. That is not to say that the aforementioned are not necessary as well. I call them the icing on the cake. There is no doubt in the fact that a wise person definitely achieves much more than a foolish one. A godly wife is constantly praying for the success of her spouse and protection from all forms of danger for her family. She takes her concerns to God in prayer – talking less about them to third parties, but praying more.

For women who knew about their spouse's promiscuity before marriage, but decided to ignore it or accept it, do not expect less from him in marriage. It is very unlikely that he would change after marriage. Most times, it gets worse. Make no mistake; you cannot change anyone, only GOD can. Complaining or crying over the issue just worsens it. Since only GOD has the ability to change anyone, you could as well take all your needs and concerns to Him in prayer.

I still strongly recommend prevention rather than cure.

9

WHEN LOVE DIES... AND WHY?

Love dies. Yes, it does. It either grows or dies.

Just like children are nurtured daily into realising their full potential, couples also need to nurture their love on a daily basis in order for it to reach its full potential. Just like children are precious, so also is love, and it should be treated as such.

> Children are tender; so also is love.
>
> Children need to be catered to; so also does love.
>
> Children need and use up plenty of our time; so also does love.
>
> Children require years to grow and develop from infancy to adulthood; so also does love.
>
> Children left unattended too soon look miserable; so also does love.

You cannot eat your cake and have it too. What exactly do you give priority to? Where do you spend most of your time? On what do you expend most of your energy? What steps are you currently taking to keep your love alive? Is the love between you and your spouse growing or dying? Think carefully about it.

Take a few seconds to imagine a garden with lovely flowers, well catered to, pruned and simply beautiful to behold. Such a garden will no doubt, be peaceful and serene. The scent that exudes from its beautifully blooming flowers will leave anyone stunned. Even the birds and the butterflies will be unable to resist their charm. That is what love between couples should feel like – irresistible, charming, beautiful, peaceful....

> Love is as beautiful and as tender as flowers.
> Love needs to be catered to, just the same way as flowers.

> Love, if abandoned for too long, will lose its vibe, just the same way as flowers in a garden abandoned for too long, would be overtaken by weeds which would eventually overtake and choke up the flowers to death. That is exactly what happens to love if left unattended to.

In essence, love should be nurtured on a daily basis. No room for lapses. Identify the weeds and root them out. Why wait for so long to identify the cause of your waning love? Renew your love for each other on a daily basis. Root out those weeds that seem to be getting in the way of your love for each other. Did I hear someone say, "Easier said than done?" Well, you have no choice; just do it! Be deliberate at it. Thresh issues out before they escalate to the point they are irresolvable. I understand that so many men are not very good at communicating effectively due to their quiet nature. Agreed! But, if your marriage is not worth the talk, go ahead and be quiet.

Selfishness seems to be a major stumbling block in most marriages. Until selflessness begins guiding the actions of couples, there might be no head way in the issue of love. Love between couples should be expressed whether you feel like it or not. Actions speak louder than words. Love should be allowed to flourish and not wane. It should be treated as a plant that must be watered daily in order for it to survive and grow to maturity. Even children, who have been catered to up to adulthood, have to take over the responsibility of their upkeep in order to remain healthy and alive. Likewise plants; they need to be cared for even after maturity. So also does love. The moment a person, a plant or even love, stops getting the necessary daily requirements for survival, it dies.

It is okay to work long hours every day in order to earn a living. That notwithstanding, the home should not suffer in anyway. Work out your schedule to include date nights when possible to make up for lost hours not spent together. It should be a crime not to spend at least two hours of the day together. It does not necessarily have to be about sex. The aim is to promote intimacy between a husband and wife on a daily basis.

Talk about anything and everything. It does not have to be something serious. If you feel talking excessively might lead to engaging in gossip, do other things together. Read Bible stories; read bedtime stories to the children together. Listen to music or watch movies together. Any activity together would do. If it is impossible to achieve spending time together during the week, I suggest you make time during the weekends. Make an effort to make it work (drop the mobile phones *wink*). Do not allow your love for each other to grow cold. Make daily rules for expressing your love for each other. You could come up with a to-do-list for your daily love activities just about the same way as that for work.

For the sake of promoting love and togetherness among members of the family, it is important to create family time together that includes the children. The feeling of love and togetherness shared between couples must be extended to the children as well. It drives home a message to the children. They will have families of their own someday. So, teach them the right way to go about it. Going to see a movie together is not a bad idea. My children love that very much. If you are unable to afford to go to the movies, you could set days aside to watch movies in the comfort of your home, pretending you are at the theater to make it more fun. Playing fun games together at home is also a good one. Reading Bible stories to them and teaching them about God is awesome. My children totally love that. Figure out other ways to promote the feeling of togetherness in the home. It is completely up to you.

When love dies, it is almost impossible to revive it. When it is only damaged, it can be revived. To revive love requires much more effort than the recommended daily requirements to keep it healthy and vital. Do the right thing!

WOMAN, WIFE, MOTHER

10

PAYING THE PRICE

Every success story has a price tag

Success in any field of endeavour does not come easily. Every successful athlete knows what it is to pay the price for success. Hours, days, weeks, months, and sometimes years of hard work are put into training. They say there is no short cut to success. Indeed there is none. Although there is no yard stick that could be used to measure the success of parenting, the end result is all that matters.

Great moms are not born, they are made. Dedication, devotion, selflessness, and hard work are the key words. What amount of dedication are you putting into being a successful mom? How much devotion and selflessness are you putting into raising your children so that they become successful and responsible individuals? How much hard work are you putting into carrying out your responsibilities as a wife and as a mom?

The other day, I took my daughter to plait her hair when I saw a child (about 2 years of age) wandering about. His diaper was obviously due for a change. The shorts he wore were extremely dirty. He had mucus running down his nostrils. He looked very unkempt. His mom owned one of the shops at the plaza where my daughter's hair was being made. One of the shop owners complained that the child always looked that way. How negligent can some mothers be? In the words of one of my Aunties, "some moms should be screened for a license to raise kids."

I see so many moms show negligence and a lack of dedication in raising their children. Sometimes, it gets to me and I almost want to smack some sense into such moms, to jolt them into carrying out their responsibilities towards their children. Let us face it and not shy away from the fact that so many children are being neglected these days. The number of missing children is on the increase today partly due to the carelessness of many moms. I am particular about mothers and not fathers caring for their children and doing it right because most children tend to spend more time with their mothers than their fathers.

Growing up (in Nigeria), I remember back then, the words of a popular newscaster, Frank Olize on the Nigerian Television Authority (N.T.A) news at 9:00pm every Sunday. He would always say, "It is nine o'clock, do you know where your children are?" I was young and at the time did not quite understand what he meant by that. It is unacceptable for parents to leave children unattended at a tender age. Children are being forced to raise themselves with no prior experience whatsoever.

I was at the local market the other day when I overheard the traders ask a young child (not sure of the sex) about the mother. Apparently, the child had strayed. I remember accompanying my mom on several occasions to the local market when I was young. I never for once, got lost. I do not want to jump to conclusions about how and why that child got lost in the first place because I do not know the circumstances surrounding the incident. Nevertheless, I remember hearing a lot of criticism of the mom. The trader, whom I was purchasing some items from, was really angry at the child's mom. She could not imagine how careless a mother could be with her own child.

There is no excuse for being careless with the gift of life entrusted to us by God. I have great admiration for moms who watch over their children at any cost. They do not see their children as a burden but as an extremely important part of their lives that they cannot do without. Whenever they have to be away from them, they ensure that their children are under the watchful eyes of very responsible individuals, preferably very close and responsible family members.

On the other hand, there are mothers who do see their children as a burden. They are always too tired to carry their children along and never really care about whom they put in charge of them. They fail to assess the character of the individuals they intend to leave their children with. I do not have anything to say to such moms, but would only hope and pray that they would come to terms with reality before it is too late.

The reality is this; a lot of assaults and child abuse – physical, sexual and emotional – take place these days. Parents, especially moms, need to be on the alert. Some people may call it being paranoid, but, the cost of foolishness and carelessness is much greater. I am not advocating that you start sniffing around people, or being fearful when people are around your children. All you need to do is to be very careful about whom you leave your children with and be very vigilant when you are in public places with your children.

Kids will not remain kids forever; they grow up really fast. Jesus Christ paid a price for us by dying on the cross for our sins that we may have eternal life. **Isaiah 53:5 (KJV) says: "But He was wounded for our transgressions, He was bruised for our iniquities..." 1st Peter 3:18 (KJV) says: "For Christ also hath once suffered for sins, the just for the unjust, that He might bring us to God, being put to death in the flesh, but quickened by the Spirit. "** He paid the greatest price a parent could ever pay for a child. What price are you willing to pay for the safety, security and upbringing of your child? Think about it!

In my opinion, no price, absolutely no price is too big to pay for a child. Children deserve utmost care from their parents. You cannot and should not be too busy to attend to the needs of your children. They have been entrusted to you by God. Think about those who are still yearning for the fruit of the womb, no offense. They are still waiting on the LORD for children of their own, yet you take for granted the ones you had on a platter of gold! How dare you!

Being successful at parenthood does not happen overnight. It is time consuming. It involves a lot of effort and commitment. Be reminded of the key words: dedication, devotion, selflessness and hard work. Do not be too tired to carry out your responsibilities as a parent. Put in your best. Go the extra mile. Do the extraordinary. Fight the good fight. At the end of it all, GOD will definitely crown your effort with an outstanding success. The fact is, when your effort yields positive results with time, you will be unable to remember the hurdles you had to cross to get there.

What price are you willing to pay for your children? Think about it!

11
LASTING FULFILLMENT

Lasting fulfillment is borne after a success story has been recorded. A lot of hard work, time and resources are put into achieving that success story. It is never effortless.

Moms have been entrusted with one of the most important jobs in the world, raising and nurturing her children. The reward of nurturing one's children is not realized overnight, but over time.

Fulfillment is a feeling of satisfaction. It is subjective. What gives satisfaction to one person may not necessarily give satisfaction to another. The question is, as a mother, what do you think would give you fulfillment that would last a life time? Think about it carefully.

It baffles me that a lot of moms trade long term fulfillment for a short term one. As your children grow up they need your guidance to get it right. Why go clubbing or partying every weekend when you are supposed to be home with them? Why do things that would constantly take you away from your children? How experienced are those you leave them with when you are away having fun or carrying out other "so-called" useful or important engagements?

Good and responsible individuals do not fall out of the sky. They are usually raised and nurtured by mothers who have put in a lot of their time, effort and resources to do it right. One would naturally enjoy the company of a good child than one improperly brought up. Do not be deceived by the false saying that you need to enjoy yourself while you still can, that is, while you are still young. At whose expense does that come? Who says you can enjoy yourself at the expense of your children? The moment you decide to become a parent, you should be prepared to live up to your responsibilities as one.

The fact is the fun can wait. Eighteen years of nurturing a child is nothing compared with over thirty years of reaping the fruits of your labor. Reaping good fruits equals enjoying the rest of your life in peace, while reaping bad fruits equals suffering the consequences of your actions and bad choices for the rest of your life in pain and torment. A person either reaps good fruits or bad ones. The choice is yours!

All things being equal, an average human being lives for about seventy years of age or more. A mom who has a child at the age of twenty-seven years, and nurtures that child to about eighteen years of age (mom is now forty-five years of age), still has about twenty-five years or more to enjoy her life or reap the fruits of her labor. After successfully executing the job of nurturing one's children to adulthood, one would naturally experience a strong feeling of satisfaction. It is an irreplaceable feeling characterized by an unending joy, happiness, inner peace and lots more. That is what I call a lasting fulfillment! It is not short term, but long term. It lasts a life time!

I know parents and have heard stories about parents who are very successful in their careers, but have dysfunctional children because they failed in their responsibilities as parents. Moreover, many of such neglected children do not have close relationship with their parents; they feel very distant in most cases. An elderly woman once shared her story about how successful she was in her career. However, she expressed regrets for failing to carry out her motherly duties towards her children. According to her, she felt very lonely in her old age because she had no close relationship with her children. She had failed to strike a balance between success in her career and success in her home. It is possible to be successful in your career without neglecting your responsibilities as a mom, because at the end of the day, the pertinent question is: what really matters most to you? Remember, you are not just raising an individual but an entire generation. To become fulfilled as a mom, takes sacrifice, and a lot of time and effort! They say Rome was not built in a day. Great moms are not born; they are made; so also are great children.

Incorporate your children into your schedule. Carry them along as you pursue your career. Attend to their daily needs personally, as much as you can. I speak to mothers especially in this regard because the onus lies on you to build your home with wisdom – wisdom from God.

At the end of it all, no one but you, mothers, are either the beneficiaries of a child's good upbringing or the victims of a child's bad/failed upbringing. A child's failed upbringing makes you a victim because in the long run, a badly brought up child results in the daily physical and mental suffering/ torture of the mom responsible for that child's upbringing. This is because for the rest of her life she would have to live with seeing her child behave irresponsibly and live a wasted life. On the other hand, a mom who did a very good job responsibly nurturing and bringing up her child experiences long lasting happiness and joy because she would live to enjoy the company and reap the good deeds of her good children for the rest of her life. **Galatians 6:7 (GNB) says: "...People will reap exactly what they sow".** If you think I am wrong, you could as well carry out your research. Take a close look at the mother of a badly nurtured child (wayward child), as well as the mother of a responsible and successful child. Which of these two moms do you think is fulfilled? Be very sincere with your answers for your own good. Consequently, which of them would you like to emulate?

Patience and perseverance are priceless virtues we must possess, among others, to achieve the great feat of raising a responsible and successful child.

We can achieve that awesome feeling of satisfaction by the grace of GOD if only we set our priorities right, taking one day at a time.

I encourage moms to be patient in carrying out their responsibilities. It is sometimes tiresome and maybe frustrating for a few. But, I would always say, the end result is what matters, not the number of hurdles you had to cross to get there. The hurdles are soon forgotten after victory is achieved. Put in your best each day. Giving up is definitely not an option. You must stand tall and strong. Fight the good fight of faith.

Basically, if you refuse or fail to learn from the bad choices and experiences of others, then other people would certainly learn from yours.

12
ACTIONS SPEAK LOUDER...

Words are just not enough! I practice what I preach.

My aim as a mother is to nurture my children's spiritual, cognitive, physical, emotional and social developments, and much more.

I am one of the few women who do not believe in abdicating sole responsibilities. That is, responsibilities exclusive to me. I personally nurture my children, together with my dear husband. I am personally involved in every area of their lives – spiritual life, social life, academics and so on. I do it because I love my children and they are my sole responsibility. I get rid of distractions that would cause divided attention. For instance, employing the services of anyone in my home would cause a lot of distractions for me. My attention would be divided between my children and the hired care giver. Distractions are things that take away your attention from the real deal. They are uncalled for. They may come in several forms. Being able to identify the cause of your distractions and doing away with them is the key to ensuring undivided attention, which is an essential requirement in raising and nurturing one's children.

Owing to the fact that we are human beings, distractions are sometimes inevitable. Being able to reduce the amount of your distractions to the barest minimum or ensuring that it is completely non-existent in your daily life would do more good than harm. Useful energy now becomes available for where it is needed. That means no more wasted energy! The fact is, most times, the biggest issue is not the amount of responsibilities we have to handle. Rather, it is failing to set our priorities right on a daily basis, what may be termed as having misplaced priorities.

It is very disheartening to see that some mothers do not just get it! Ignorance is no excuse for failing to carry out your responsibilities the way you ought to. It is upsetting to witness certain nonchalant attitudes exhibited by some mothers in executing their sole responsibilities towards their children. It is very unfair to these children. They did not ask to be brought forth into the world. Rather, you chose to bring them forth. Being more sensitive to the needs of your children is not too much for you to do. **Psalms 127:3 (GNB) says: "Children are a gift from the LORD; they are a real blessing."** How do you treat a reward or a gift? Not just any reward or gift, but a very special one. Do you cherish it, misuse it or throw it away? Think about it carefully. What gift or reward in your possession means the world to you? Put differently, what possession do you presently own that means a lot to you? Guess what? Your children are worth more than that gift or possession you cherish so much. Bottom line, we should love and cherish our children while fulfilling our obligations towards them. We have no other choice than to do just that!

Psalms 19:7 (GNB) says: "The law of the LORD is perfect; it gives new strength. The commands of the LORD are trustworthy, giving wisdom to those who lack it." Wisdom from GOD is all we need. It is what makes the difference in the quality of motherhood exhibited by moms who possess it. I am extremely grateful to GOD for giving me the wisdom to go about motherhood the right way, hence this book, inspired by GOD.

This chapter has been deliberately included to show case the motherhood experiences of two resilient moms who have begun counting their blessings because they chose not to abdicate their sole responsibilities but to personally see to the upbringing of their children; doing away largely with external influences such as the hiring of domestic workers. In recent times, domestic workers have become a major source of distraction in most homes. Although, a few others still believe otherwise, time will tell. The term "domestic worker," as used above, refers to someone employed to carry out domestic chores. However, most times, these workers do not just carry out domestic chores; they are also made to carry out the "sole responsibilities" of many moms – too bad!

It is my great pleasure to briefly write about the motherhood experiences so far, of these two resilient moms; Mrs Lisa and Mrs Sasha (not real names), who both reside in the city most people describe as the busiest city in Nigeria, Lagos. It fills my heart with great joy that they both understand the need to make sacrifices, the prices they have to pay, the time and effort they have to invest in order to produce responsible, stable and successful individuals.

Mrs Lisa is the wife of a military man and a mother of three male children. For those who are very familiar with the routine of military men as well as men of the armed forces in general, you may have noticed that they hardly get to spend ample time with their families. They are away most times and only get to see their families occasionally. For these men, it is duty first, before other things, including their own family.

Mrs Lisa is a journalist by profession. In her own words, "Motherhood is beautiful, but it comes with a lot of sacrifices." While growing up, she had dreams, and spent many nights pondering on how to actualize her dreams. As a teenager at the University, she deprived herself of some pleasures so as not to lose focus. She did obtain the necessary qualifications and got married afterwards. Her journey into motherhood began. Her story...

"I started as a media officer at a Marketing Communication Agency. Due to the nature of my spouse's job, he was not resident in the same city as I was. Thus, trying to juggle between my career and my responsibilities as a wife was not very easy.

What made it even more difficult was when I started having children. I resigned and took up a more flexible job that did not have a fixed time schedule; but required a lot of movement. In the long run, it was still not favourable for my children because they were just toddlers. I always felt very exhausted after work. I thought to myself, my children need a lot of nurturing, my job needs to be attended to and my husband needs my love and attention, which I was struggling to give. I was left with no other option than to choose between my career and my family. It was a tough decision though. At first, I wanted to be selfish. I really loved my job; but on the other hand, my husband and children craved for my attention. Then, I remembered my mother and the sacrifices she made to make me who I am today. She was always there for me despite my father's absence from home due to the nature of his job, similar to that of my husband. My mom stood in the gap and ensured that my siblings and I were properly raised. Just like my mom, I wanted to be there for my children in order to instill the right values in them, to share in their moments of joy and pain; and most importantly, to be the support system that my family needs. To that effect, I quit my job. Today, I am glad I did.

"Many thought I was crazy, some felt I was stupid, a few others applauded me. To be honest with you, it is very boring being a full time housewife if you are an intellectual. Besides, it made me financially dependent on my husband. Although my husband is a good husband and father, I still wanted financial freedom. I thought of what to do that would not demand so much of my time but be financially rewarding. I am still holding on to my dreams. When the children are old enough, I would certainly go back to building my career.

"At the moment, I am focused on raising and nurturing my children. I am not just a mother to my children; I am also a teacher, a friend and a confidant. I know their strengths and weaknesses. I instill my own values in them, making them the gentlemen they should be. As time went on, I realised what I would have missed out on if I had not taken that bold step very early on in their lives. Although some mothers may have some financial challenges and may not be able to quit their jobs, but I believe that a more flexible job will give you the opportunity to care for your children the way you ought to. Absolutely no one can love your children the way you would. Paying close attention to your children would help you know when things go wrong academically, health wise, socially and psychologically. It helps you tackle the problem of juvenile delinquency and deviant behaviours very early. Most cases of teenage pregnancies and drug addiction could easily be avoided if only we took up our responsibilities the way we ought to.

"Parenting demands a lot of sacrifices. As mothers, no matter the situation we find ourselves in, we have an obligation towards our children. Money is not all there is to life. Money is good, but it is better to have well behaved and stable children in order to be at peace at retirement. As for me, I can confidently say that I am gradually reaping the fruits of my labor. Teachers who have taught my children always commend me on how well behaved they are. They are academically sound and focused young men to the glory of God.

"A word of advice to mothers out there: A lot of people will tag you as being lazy, subservient, oppressed, a fool or a weakling, simply because you decided to quit your job in order to stay back home to care for your children. It could be depressing to say the least. Your 'so-called' friends would distance themselves from you. They would look down on you and make you feel really bad about yourself. If you lack self-worth, it could get to you and lead to an inferiority complex. People would flaunt their success and wealth in your face, forgetting that money is not everything. Instead of love and understanding, you get mockery. Some may understand how much sacrifice you had to make; many others will not. It does not matter what challenges you face, it is only a matter of time.

"My final words: The society places too much emphasis on wealth. Only those who are wealthy are accorded much more respect and admiration. No one is paying attention to the causes of societal ills and decadence, nor promoting the right values, norms and ethics. It is extremely tough on those who decide to make these sorts of sacrifices; even some husbands belittle their spouses sometimes. Women who suspend their careers or ambition for the sake of raising and nurturing their children should be encouraged and helped to actualize their dreams once the children have come of age. Losing self-worth is a catalyst to depression, and the consequences could be fatal. Therefore, let us applaud these individuals and support their cause for a better society and value system."

Mrs Sasha works in a Non-Governmental Organisation (NGO). She is a mother of four children. Her story....

"Initially I had a very demanding job which involved travelling a lot. I travelled a lot even while having my children. After a while, it became difficult to travel around with my children, so I decided to take up a job in an N.G.O. It was much more flexible, and it afforded me more time for my children. I could not become a full time house wife due to the financial responsibilities I had towards my extended family. I am also a free-lance consultant. In as much as I needed to earn a living, I also needed to raise and nurture my children personally.

"Motherhood involves a lot of sacrifices. I make it a point of duty to be there for my children. I am personally involved in the day to day activities of my children. I teach them personally, helping them with their homework. I have never employed the services of a teacher by way of extra lessons. Personal hygiene is very important to me. They are actively involved in doing the house chores. I made washing their clothes so much fun by involving everyone in that particular activity at the same time. We would sit around in the laundry room together to do our washing. Most importantly, I teach them the word of God, a weapon they would need to weather any storm.

"Due to the close relationship I have with my children, I was able to discover their individual talents, which I helped them develop. My younger son is very skilful at playing the organ. He is currently a member of the choir at the Church we attend. He is also a writer. My six year old daughter teaches two to three year old children, and is being paid for it. My older son is an author of two books. He was a valedictorian and got a partial scholarship to study at one of the best high schools in Nigeria.

"It has certainly not been a bed of roses, but I have no regrets whatsoever. I had to put structures in place to help in the developmental process of my children. Today, as a result of my well behaved children and their academic achievements so far, people ask for my help in coaching their children. It is amazing to see the outpour of love and kindness I am currently receiving from everyone around me. Preceding the departure of my older son to high school, a group of people flooded my apartment just to bid him farewell. I was speechless. I am extremely happy and I have peace of mind.

"My candid advice to mothers out there is that: money is not everything. Presently, I live in a small apartment, but I know that at the right time, I would have sufficient money at my disposal. It is very important to set your priorities right early enough in order to reap the full benefits in later years."

I sincerely hope that every mom out there would be inspired by the motherhood experiences of these two exceptional moms. I must commend the effort of many other moms out there who are doing a fantastic job at raising and nurturing their children the right way. It gladdens my heart whenever I come across such moms. Keep being great moms and never settle for less. **Nehemiah 8:10 (GNB) says: "...The joy that the LORD gives you will make you strong."**

Remember, nothing is impossible to a willing heart, and most importantly; **Philippians 4:13 (KJV) says: "I can do all things through Christ who strengthens me."**

CONCLUSION

I strongly believe that every woman who reads this book will be inspired in one way or another to work towards becoming the woman she was created to be; a great wife and mom, while also fulfilling her God-given purpose to humanity. As you begin to understand the purpose of your existence, you will begin to unravel the very essence of your being.

Moms have been specially created to handle various circumstances without being torn apart. Do not for once doubt your God-given abilities to pull through this life-long journey of motherhood. Remember, GOD chose you! As challenging as motherhood may be or seem to be, never lose focus on the reason for your existence. Always bear in mind that every living being has been created to fulfill a specific purpose and subsequently, has been empowered by the creator (GOD), to adequately fulfill that purpose. Being able to discover the purpose of one's existence is no doubt the first and most important step towards fulfilling that purpose. Having unravelled the purpose of your existence, fulfilling it is entirely up to you. You could either go ahead and fulfill the purpose or shy away from it. Whichever path you choose, always bear in mind that at the end of time, everyone will surely give account of his or her stewardship to our creator (GOD).

With a wonderfully loving spouse and amazing children to spend a lifetime with, with so much to achieve as a wife and as a mom, with a growing knowledge of yourself and your abilities in progress and with so many contributions to make towards the betterment of the lives around you, you will definitely be filled with the motivation to go through each day, and of course with the right attitude as well. In addition, never ever stop developing yourself into a much better person, and stop considering giving up because of the enormous challenges that come with motherhood. Motherhood

CONCLUSION

is for a lifetime, so learn to relax and live one day at a time. Begin now by drawing out a plan or schedule that will help you through each day. You must have a plan to help you into becoming a great mom. Do not just sit there and live like someone without a purpose. You have been given the ability and the opportunity, so utilize them judiciously and fulfill your purpose to the best of your ability. I have not said the road would be easy, but by the grace of God, it is achievable.

Finally, if only moms could learn to perceive motherhood as it really is; beautiful, rewarding, fulfilling, worthwhile and much more, they would be able to happily embrace the role regardless of its challenges. Stop pointing fingers at others for your predicament and comparing your situation to those of others. Personalize the experiences that come with motherhood and make it work for you. From now on, commit yourself to making motherhood and whatever situation you are presently in work to your advantage and not to your disadvantage. **John**

14:16 (GNB) says: I will ask the Father, and He will give you another Helper, who will stay with you forever." GOD has given us the Holy Spirit to stay with us *"forever."* Therefore, take hold of this great promise and ask the Holy Spirit for help in time of need, knowing that He is always with you.

I have definitely taken hold of this great promise of God to send me a helper and the opportunity given to me by Him. I am often asked the question, how do you do it without any (physical) help? Yes, I used the word "physical," because I have a helper who has been appointed to me divinely by GOD. As for me, the grace of God is more than sufficient to successfully see me through this life changing journey of motherhood as well as, the entire journey of my life.

What about you? What is your story? Better still, what do you want your story to entail? The choice is yours!

www.ingramcontent.com/pod-product-compliance
Lightning Source LLC
LaVergne TN
LVHW051835080426
835512LV00018B/2886